C000224799

Great Yarmouth & Gorleston

A Pictorial History

Two young girls paddle in the sea on the beach near Britannia Pier in 1908.

Great Yarmouth & Gorleston

A Pictorial History

Cliff Richard Temple

Phillimore

1993

Published by
PHILLIMORE & CO. LTD.
Shopwyke Manor Barn, Chichester, Sussex

© Cliff Richard Temple, 1993

ISBN 0 85033 854 9

Printed and bound in Great Britain by
BIDDLES LTD.
Guildford, Surrey

List of Illustrations

Frontispiece: Young girls paddling, 1908

Introduction

During the fifth century a small sandbank formed itself from the sea, began to increase in size and became firm land. Fishermen found it an ideal place for drying their nets. Then in the year A.D.495, Cerdic, a Saxon prince, landed there, with the crews of five of his ships, and named it Cerdic Shore. In 1008 dwellings were erected at the highest part and called 'Fullers Hill', no doubt named after the first fisherman to build a house there.

The earliest reference to Yarmouth is in Domesday Book, where it is recorded as having a population of one hundred. This new 'town', being the easternmost point, quickly increased in population due to the arrival of foreigners from Holland, France and Norway, and soon it was to become the most flourishing sea port on this part of the English coast. By the middle of the 13th century, the humble herring became the favourite food with everybody, from the king himself to his most humble peasants.

By then, Yarmouth had acquired a certain degree of importance so that its inhabitants thought it advisable to take precautions and provide for its defence. Thus, in 1261, Henry III gave permission for the building of a town wall. On 28 September 1262, work commenced; but alas it took 111 years to complete. One of the reasons for delay being the terrible Black Death which struck the town in 1349 and claimed the lives of 7,000 people out of a population of nine thousand.

The wall was seven feet thick and 23 feet high, built round three sides of the town and backing on to the river. It was 2,280 yards in length, including 16 towers and 10 gates. In fact, it was almost a garrison. The people were confined within these walls, which resulted in houses being packed very closely together. Thus were originated the famous 'Yarmouth Rows', 145 in number and likened by Charles Dickens to a 'grid-iron'. Most of them were named, either after nearby pubs, adjacent roads, or local notables. A well-known row was 'Kitty Witches' which only measured 30 inches in width at one end. To traverse these narrow thoroughfares special carts were built, called troll-carts, one for passengers and the other for merchandise deliveries. An unusual feature was the shafts which were fitted outside the wheels, making it easier to gauge whether the cart was narrow enough to enter a street. The Yarmouth Rows are quite unique in English history although, owing to the many raids by German aircraft, very few are left.

The fine church of St Nicholas was built in 1101 by Herbert de Losinga, the Bishop of Norwich and, as the town increased in prosperity, so the church increased in size. By the 19th century it was claimed to be the largest parish church in England.

Yarmouth also had, and still has, some other very fine and ancient buildings, not the least being the Tollhouse of 1260, once used as a Court of Justice, and now as a museum. A 'showpiece' house is that of 4 South Quay, built in 1596 by Benjamin Cooper, which has a panelled drawing room with an elaborate plaster ceiling and some fine period rooms. According to tradition, it is the place where the execution of Charles I was decided upon in 1648. John Carter, the owner of the house at that time, was a friend of Cromwell, as was Miles Corbet, who was one of the signatories of Charles' death warrant. The Custom House on the South Quay was built as a private house in 1720 and is now a survivor of the enemy bombing. In 1702 the almshouses, now called the Fishermen's hospital (a cluster of small cottages in a courtyard) were built for 'decayed fishermen' who could end their days in comparative comfort. In 1714 St George's church was built in the style of Wren's churches and paid for by a special tax on imports of coal into the port.

Yarmouth's quayside was a perfect picture, lined with trees for the whole length and described by Defoe as the 'finest quay in England or Europe' (*Tour of Eastern England, 1722*). There would be a large amount of shipping in the river with fishing vessels, brigs, wherries, barques and schooners unloading produce from distant shores, whilst in later years paddle-wheel tugs plied their trade and towed large sailing vessels in and out of the harbour. Even at the beginning of the century (1913) there would be nearly two thousand sailing and steam fishing craft in harbour on Sunday for the Sabbath rest. So busy had Yarmouth become, that it was the premier herring fishing port in the world.

Yarmouth also has a great naval history and in the 14th century its naval strength was greater than that of any port in England, including London. In fact, in 1337, Yarmouth had a navy of its own, comprising 20 men-of-war and called Yarmouth Navy, and the harbour became the Scapa Flow for the English fleet! Yarmouth was also one of the chief gateways to the Continent. Such a conspicuous part was played by Yarmouth throughout the war with France, sending out 42 ships and 1,075 men, that Edward III granted the Royal Arms to be added to those of the Borough.

In 1799 Admiral Duncan took over the fleet anchored in the Yarmouth Roads (a safe passageway between dangerous sandbanks and shore) and on 3 October he sailed from the Roads to defeat the Dutch fleet off Camperdown, returning to Yarmouth with seven of the Dutch ships as prizes. To commemorate this victory, a new terrace of houses near the Wellington Pier was named Camperdown. Incidentally, it was Admiral Duncan who had earlier captured the famous French frigate *Lutine*, whose bell is now rung at Lloyd's of London when an important announcement is to be made. The *Lutine* was added to the fleet of George III in 1799, when she started on her final and ill-fated trip from Yarmouth Roads, laden with bullion worth about three million pounds, and was wrecked.

From the time of Edward III to that of Edward VI, the Admiralty considered Yarmouth opinion of paramount importance as a guide to their designers, and later, when Lord Fisher was at the Admiralty, it was the custom to send all the important ships to Yarmouth Roads so that the local magnates, shipwrights and seamen could pass judgement on their appearance, and probable effectiveness. Clearly the port of Yarmouth richly deserves its status as a secondary Cinque Port as well as its full name of Great Yarmouth.

Windmills

The casual visitors coming to Great Yarmouth for the first time, thinking it is just a popular holiday resort with a one-time flourishing fishing industry, would never in their wildest dreams associate the town with that beautifier of the countryside – the windmill. At one time Great Yarmouth had the tallest windmill in England. Known as

High Mill, or sometimes Press's Mill, it was 122 ft. high and its lantern at the top made it 135 ft. high. It consisted of 11 storeys and was built in 1892. So large was the base of the mill – 46 ft. in diameter – that a road-way passed right through it, enabling farmer's carts to pass, load and unload inside the mill. It was of the 'tower' variety and its revolving cap, which carried the five-ton windshaft, the sails, fan-tail and fly-stage, weighed 15 tons. The mill worked both day and night; a double shift of four men each was worked. In 1854 (during the Crimean War) the mill came into national prominence when its flour was supplied to Lord Raglan's army and shipped by a number of Yarmouth's famous clipper schooners, chartered to race to the Black Sea ports. It had various owners – B. H. Press being the last from 1845. The windmill continued to make wholemeal flour until 1892, when it was used for grist only. Work ceased in 1898.

On the death of Mr. Press (in 1904), the mill was auctioned off, and although it had cost £10,000 to build, it was knocked down for £100. The bricks from it were used to build a whole row of terraced houses, and the spot on which the mill stood is indicated by the houses having red chimney pots, the others being of stone colour. The noticeable red pots are at 35 and 36 High Mill Terrace, Gatacre Road.

Near the High Mill stood another well-known mill called the Green Cap (from the colour of its cap or 'top'). It had an adjoining granary plus a pigeon loft, and when it caught fire it is reported that bystanders saw the poor pigeons flying from the burning mill with their wings on fire.

A short journey away there still stands the famous Berney Arms windmill which can only be visited by boat and railway and has been taken over by the Ministry of Works for Preservation. It once ground Breydon mud and sea shells to make a mortar for building the adjacent river walls – a custom, it is said, the Romans used when building Burgh Castle. Once again of the 'tower' variety, the mill wears a true 'Norfolk boat' cap.

The only windmill left in Great Yarmouth is at Ash Tree Farm, which was working until its sails blew off in the 1953 hurricane.

The Seaside and Holiday Entertainment

It may seem strange that the popularity of the seaside owes its origin to a doctor who, in 1750, wrote a pamphlet advocating that salt water could be a cure for every ailment, and could be taken both internally and externally. It was thought to be good for asthma, tuberculosis, deafness and even cancer. Within ten years, a trip to the seaside had become essential for fashionable society; what had been the pursuit of only a few, had now become a craze, especially after King George III took a dip in the 'briny' at Weymouth.

In 1759 Yarmouth joined the throng by erecting a bath-house near the sea. A public reading room was then added, where 'London papers were on sale – daily!'. Later came the balls, parties and breakfasts.

As the 18th-century ladies objected to the nude bathing that took place, Benjamin Beale invented the bathing machine – a hut on four wheels. This contrivance was pulled into the sea by horses; the would-be bather could then enter the sea by steps, protected from viewers by a canvas hood, and bathe in complete privacy.

In Edwardian times, it would not have been August without the traditional trip to Yarmouth for a dip in the sea. Restricted by the fashions of the day – boaters and starched collars for men, and long flowing dress for women – prospective bathers could not do much more than 'dip'. In spite of the glare and warmth of the sun on those long summer days, the tradition was style and its essence, decorum.

Top of the bill for Yarmouth holiday-makers, however, was listening to a band playing in the Wellington Gardens, and a social 'must' was for young men and women (who had to be seen) to promenade along the winding pathways (getting a date?), whilst taking in the sounds of the classics or musical comedies of the era. A thrill for some was the Revolving Tower. This was a steel girder affair, some 144 ft. high, in which a 'cage' revolved on the outside, thus enabling people to stand in one position and view the whole of Yarmouth and the surrounding countryside. It was even possible to see Norwich Cathedral, some twenty miles away.

Great Yarmouth has always had many forms of entertainment. Until a few years ago, it had a theatre exactly the same age as the world famous La Scala in Milan, built in 1778. The theatre was hailed for its magnificence, prices being three shillings for a box, one shilling for the gallery, and its opening gave 'Theatre Plain' its name. The Theatre Royal was famed for its plays, but it closed in 1928, the site remaining empty until the opening of the Regal in 1934.

On the seafront stood one of the earliest buildings erected in Britain for the sole purpose of showing films. The Gem opened in 1908 and was managed by C. B. Cochran, who later became famous as 'Cocky' the impresario. In those early days there was segregation of the sexes and the men sat on one side of the cinema, with the women on the other. There was a 1,200 tip-up seat capacity.

The Hippodrome was built in 1903 and had a sunken ring. It was mainly a circus, with horses, lions and trapeze artists, and usually the perfomance finished with the ring being flooded with water and aquatic spectacles being performed therein. A favourite act was the 'Red Indian' saga, where red indians, high up in the gods, waved their arms and brandished their tomahawks, whilst making wild war whoops as they plunged over the 'waterfall' after the hero and heroine, only to capsize their flimsy canoes in the inky waters of the 'lake' beneath.

Opening on Boxing Day, 1914, the Regent was a superb piece of design. It was equipped for films and stage-shows and accommodated 1,679 patrons, 50 of whom could pay for boxes. By contrast the Royal Aquarium is often referred to as being Yarmouth's greatest mistake. The reason for this is that its structure has blocked what would have been a fine view of the whole length of Yarmouth's long frontage. As an aquarium it failed, and, converted into a theatre, becoming 'royal' after the patronage of King Edward VII when he was Prince of Wales. Many plays were performed there, but it really came into its own with the arrival of popular musical comedies from America in the 1920s. These productions simply 'filled the house'; first-class companies came from London to perform. When amusement fashions changed, films were shown and eventually the Royal Aquarium had the first Cinemascope screen (a new wide screen in colour showing 'talkies') in East Anglia.

Following the Regent's opening on Boxing Day, the Yarmouth market-place Central opened on Easter Monday, 5 April 1915, showing many fine films and giving a stage performance in the interval. It changed its name in the 1930s to the Plaza and closed in the 1950s. Finally, it was demolished and in its place stands Woolworth's store.

A popular cinema on the Marine Parade, specialising in cowboy films with W. S. Hart and Eddie Polo, is still going strong. It gained fame a few years back by displaying at its entrance a brass plaque, which described how the cinema was hit by a shell from a German warship in 1916.

At Gorleston the Coliseum was opened in the High Street on August Bank Holiday, 1913. It was a popular place of entertainment for those living south of the river, until it closed down in 1970 and was finally demolished. The Palace was built in the High Street, Gorleston, in 1939 and became a bingo hall in 1964. Situated near Gorleston Pier and the swimming pool, the Pavilion was used for a multitude of entertainments. Taken over by George Gilbert, of circus fame, in 1908, it provided films, vaudeville and music hall.

Throughout the summer holiday season, both Britannia and Wellington Piers vied with each other to give the best performances. Between 1912 and 1915 Pierrots were the fashion, dressed in white, with a dunce's hat and black pom-poms, and they gave quite lively shows. Later, radio stars were to take their place.

Great Yarmouth acquired a bargain when its Corporation bought Torquay's Winter Garden for £1,300. Decorated with palms and hanging baskets of flowers and ferns, the garden adorned a fine skating rink, but skating was not a profitable venture, so it was eventually converted into an Alpine Biergarten with appropriate painted scenery and colourful umbrellas. It certainly added enchantment to the ornate bandstand in the Wellington Gardens. During the Second World War, however, the bandstand was demolished and the spacious grounds were turned into a zoo. The remaining area became a skating rink. A model village is now on this site.

During the 1920s a favourite haunt for youngsters was Barron's Amusement Arcade on the 'front'. This boasted a roundabout, a switchback railway, waxworks, shooting gallery and 'chamber of horrors'. One character to be found on the beach (who always drew a good audience) was Madame Cook, a phrenologist who had an uncanny gift for reading one's character, and always drew a good audience.

The 1920s also saw the emergence of a sandbank, now known as Scroby Sandbank. In no time at all, terns, gulls, wild fowl and seals made it their new home, and many shipwrecks, previously concealed by the sea, could be seen once again. The Yarmouth boatmen were quick to seize the opportunity to take holiday-makers out to the island to see the wrecks and seals, and to gather the birds' eggs (an activity now prohibited). Men gathered eggs in hatfuls, but regretted it later if some got smashed, as a vile, fishy stench emanated from them. In 1927, the *Cambria*, a large beach sailing vessel, landed a party of between thirty and forty people on the sandbank. However, when it was time to leave, the boat was found to be stuck fast in the sand. Every available motor boat was summoned to help the vessel, ropes were secured and a tug-of-war commenced between the twenty or so motor boats and the grip of Scroby Sandbank. With the rising tide the boats won and the *Cambria* returned to shore with a number of frightened passengers.

Maritime

Being nearer to the Continent than it is to London, Great Yarmouth is a useful and convenient port for many ships from many nations. In its heyday, Yarmouth had cargoes of timber arriving from Baltic ports. There would be 'square-sail' brigs, barques and large schooners, their decks simply overflowing with balks of timber to be unloaded at the quayside and the massive timber yards alongside the river. Both the warehouses and quays are empty today and a timber-carrying ship is a rare sight. Collier brigs, too, would bring tons of coal for Bessey & Palmer (the local coal merchants established for 200 years), to be loaded into waggons which were pulled by a little steam engine to the coal yards. A frequent sight was to see 'Johnny Onionman' descending the gangway of a Dutch sailing vessel with a string of Spanish onions suspended from a long pole on his shoulder, which he used to hawk round the various Rows and dwellings. He would be dressed in a brownish colour smock, corduroy trousers, clogs and a red-spotted kerchief. A treat for the locals was when a cargo of casks of wine were unloaded and a cask fell from the crane. All would make a rush to fill their bellies with what was left inside the split cask.

Being such a busy port, it was inevitable that some of Yarmouth's ships should come to grief. Ships were stranded on the dreaded sandbanks (just a mile or so from the foreshore), ran aground during fog and even caught fire. It is recorded that in the latter half of the 19th century 40,000 trading vessels passed through Yarmouth Roads every year, while 1,400 ships are known to have been 'sheltered' in these Roads at the same time. At the turn of the century there were 27 R.N.L.I. lifeboat stations between Aldeburgh in Suffolk and Hunstanton in Norfolk, which is approximately one lifeboat station to every four miles of coastline. The old wooden vessels in the days of sail were very vulnerable to the vagaries of all weathers. In fact, the well-advertised 'Golden Sands of Yarmouth', so beloved by the summer holiday-maker, were far from golden to the ship-owner and unfortunate seaman. Yarmouth had a fine lifeboat station situated on the Front which contained two lifeboats, and when the occasion arose a boat would be launched by many willing hands on an errand of mercy. Taking into consideration 'private' lifeboats, there were as many as six lifeboats on duty at Yarmouth and Gorleston between 1883 and 1892.

One 'private' lifeboat, however, had a bad record for capsizing; it was the *Rescuer* which turned over in 1866 with a loss of 13 men from the 16-strong crew. In 1867 it was involved in a collision which caused several of her crew to drown. In 1888 another private boat, the *Refuge*, crashed into the North Bank after rescuing the crew of a steamship with the loss of four lives. Miss Elizabeth Simpson Stone had a new lifeboat built at Yarmouth and presented it to the Gorleston Rangers to replace the *Rescuer*. The vessel was named after her, *Elizabeth Simpson*, and during 51 years' service she never capsized, lost any of her crew nor lost a 'guest'. She was launched 119 times and saved 441 lives. The *Elizabeth Simpson* is still going strong, having been converted to a private passenger boat which takes holidaymakers for river trips on the Norfolk Broads.

The first R.N.L.I. lifeboat to be stationed at Gorleston was the *Leicester* in 1886. She was subscribed for by the citizens of Leicester on hearing of the loss of life when the *Rescuer* capsized. Not only did the citizens pay for the boat, but they also provided the money to build a lifeboat shed as well.

A capsize which shocked the whole of the East Coast occurred in November 1901 when flares were seen from the Barber Sands, so attempts were therefore made to launch the Caister lifeboat, *Beauchamp*. At the first attempt she was knocked off her skids by heavy seas, and had to be recovered for another attempt. She finally got away, but before long cries were heard and men raced to the spot only to see the lifeboat had been driven ashore and had capsized. Within seconds men jumped into the raging surf to rescue the rescuers but only managed to recover three bodies. The sea later relinquished eight bodies, but the ninth it retained. The *Beauchamp* was salvaged from the sea but was never used again as a lifeboat. She was sold and spent the rest of her working life as a cruiser on the Norfolk Broads. A few years ago, she was retired and presented to Caister as a possible museum piece, but they refused to have her and she was sent to Gorleston where she lay rotting. Finally it was decided to burn her, and she finished as a funeral pyre.

The red-sailed London and Rochester barges were frequent visitors to Yarmouth and these 'maids of all work', like their larger 'sisters', also came to grief. This mostly happened when they were riding out a storm, being at anchor in the Roads. A sudden gale would spring up and cause the vessels to drag anchors and finally drift ashore into the breakers. This happened to the *Scotia* on 7 October 1929 and it became a total wreck.

Yarmouth has seen two fiery spectacles, one being the steamer *Oscar* which caught fire whilst proceeding to the port. Her cargo consisted of 2,500 loads of deals, battens and boards and the fire soon spread through this, rapidly overtaking the whole vessel, the boat becoming a flaming torch. The crew of 23, in the meantime, had taken to the ship's boats to be picked up by the Gorleston lifeboat. Tugs sent to quench the flames were unsuccessful and the fire remained burning for four days and nights. Twenty-foot high piles of burnt timber formed on the beach. Finally, Trinity House sent a tender to the scene, floated a charge of explosives on a raft to her and the wreck went down within twenty minutes!

The second 'sight of a lifetime' was that of a fire aboard another steamship, the *Porthcawl*. Laden with 2,000 tons of esparto grass she remained burning for nearly a week. The glow of the burning vessel in the darkness lit up the faces of the thousands of sightseers who gathered on the Promenade to witness the unusual sight of a ship on fire so close at hand. Yarmouth's boatmen had the time of their lives, taking out visitors and getting as close to the heat as they dared. The fire burnt itself out and a tug pushed the vessel to the foreshore, where she lay, just twisted metal and with only the funnel still standing. Eventually, she was pumped out, patched up and towed away by a salvage tug to the ship breakers.

Perhaps the most amazing, or even frightening, sight was when the sailing barque *Erna* dragged her anchors and came ashore on 11 November 1905. As the ship fell apart, hundreds of rats scuttled out of her and plunged into the sea. They swam ashore in droves, all frantically making for the safety of the beach. Most of them reached the shore and, at one time, a patch of the beach was black with them. Very few spectators were inclined to stand in their way.

On 4 November 1902 an iron-constructed schooner, the *Maggie Williams*, arrived off Yarmouth from Dublin. In the rapidly deteriorating weather the skipper tried to run his ship into harbour without the usual pilot. The vessel missed her helm and crashed into the old Dutch Pier at Gorleston. The crew was hauled to the safety of the pier but the captain remained missing. A Gorleston lifeboatman was lowered to the deck and found the captain sitting in his bunk smoking a pipe, intent on going down with his ship. After much persuasion and on realising that the lifeboatman had risked his life to save him, the captain consented to change his mind and was hauled to safety.

In October 1903 the first homogeneous ('homo') type battleships were sent to the Yarmouth Roads and were lined up off the same jetty on which Nelson landed after winning the Battle of the Nile in 1800. They were H.M.S. *Majestic, Mars, Jupiter, Prince George, Hannibal, Sutles, Doris, Prometheus* and *Magnificent*, and they drew thousands of sightseers to the Promenade. During the First World War the Monitor H.M.S. *Roberts* was based near the Fish Wharf at Yarmouth and, on one occasion when its huge 16-in. gun was fired, half the windows in Gorleston were shattered! More modern vessels which have paid Yarmouth a visit include 'The Four Rs': H.M.S. *Resolution, Royal Oak* (the first warship sunk by the enemy in the Second World War), *Ramilies* and *Revenge* – four monsters all anchored off Britannia Pier. Then came the singles:

H.M.S. *Warspite*, the grand old lady of Narvik fame, *Repulse*, probably the largest and longest vessel Yarmouth has ever seen, being 794 ft. 2½ in. long, 102 ft. beam and 27 ft. draught and of 36,800 tons loaded weight. Yarmouth also had visits from the three-funnelled *Norfolk* which gained undying fame by being the first vessel to score a hit during the battle with the German *Scharnhorst*, and helping to hunt and destroy the *Bismark*. She was followed by the aircraft carrier *Furious*, which drew more sightseers than any other vessel, then the destroyers *Soleby*, *Saintes*, *Troubridge* and *Defender*. On 17 July 1970 Yarmouth saw the arrival of the newest guided missile destroyer H.M.S. *Norfolk*, which unlike its namesake's turret and huge guns, carried instead the Seaslug guided missile and was at that time the most modern vessel in the world.

In 1960 Yarmouth was delighted when a very modern frigate made its appearance off the Britannia Pier, as the vessel was named after the town, H.M.S. *Yarmouth*, being the sixth of the Yarmouth line, was commissioned, ready for action, in March 1960 and visited the town in July of that year. She was the largest anti-submarine frigate to be built for the Royal Navy. On her last visit to the town, on 8 July 1984, the Freedom of the Borough was bestowed upon the ship. In the hot sunshine people turned out in their thousands to see the official ceremony and the colourful parade which followed. The band of the Royal Anglian Regiment provided the music and the mayor, in civic red and ermine, took the salute and inspected the ship's company. It was the parade through the streets that thrilled the public as the company exercised their right to 'parade with swords drawn, bayonets fixed, colours flying, bands playing and drums beating'. It was a freedom festival of which to be proud.

The Advent of North Sea Oil and Gas

By a quirk of fate the North Sea provides not only fish but also the wherewithal to cook it – namely gas. A complete reformation has taken place at Great Yarmouth. Plots of land which had become vacant owing to a diminishing fishing industry were bought up, and old factories and fishing premises altered or demolished and new buildings were erected. Broken quays were repaired and strengthened, the fish wharves were done away with, as were the pickling and curing establishments. Where once one could walk on the South Denes to see ships sailing upriver, it is now wired off and warehouses, sheds and buildings populate the area.

In its long history as a port, Yarmouth had never before seen such a collection of strange-looking craft as that which, suddenly and without much warning, entered its two and a half miles of river. Townsmen on the pier searching the horizon were amazed to see a weird contraption of masts and derricks being towed in their direction. It was the 3,000-ton American oil rig, the *Glomar IV*, which was to drill the first exploration well for Gulf Oil off the coast of Norfolk. The *Avoyelles*, which helped to tow the rig across the Atlantic, had a very low free-board, which bemused the tug men.

At first oil was not found in any quantity, but another valuable product was – namely gas. Great Yarmouth became the base, and every week a new, completely different vessel arrived. The inhabitants were used to seeing black-hulled ships, but these new arrivals were painted yellow or brilliant blue, green or a multi-colour of green, white and black. Soon Yarmouth river had almost the same number of ships as her previous fishing fleet. So numerous where they that all the mooring sites were occupied, and fishing craft had to seek fresh grounds nearer to the town centre. Soon huge pipes appeared on the quays, ready to be transported to a factory for bitumen treatment for their final sea-bed resting place. Strange-looking monsters with a host of pipes were used for making a bed 10 ft. deep at the bottom of the sea for the treated pipes to carry gas from the rig to the shore. Then came the 'revolution' – every household had their gas cookers altered from burning coal gas to the new-found product.

Oil was then found and more rigs made their appearance. Each costing about five million pounds, the rigs vary in appearance, but fundamentally consist of an enormous platform on long legs, upon which huge derricks rear up to the heavens. Apart from the numerous oil companies which have taken possession of the Yarmouth Denes and quayside, many other firms have moved into premises for the supply of casing and pipes, chemicals, materials for drilling mud, tanks and pumps. An air base has also been built to house the large helicopters which fly principals and crews to the rigs and back.

1. This watercolour by C. J. W. Winter shows the ancient North Gate from inside the walls. Construction of the ramparts began in the reign of Henry III and took 130 years to complete. The gate, after which the present Northgate Street was named, was removed in 1807.

2. The North-West Tower is one of the few remaining towers of the medieval walls which surrounded Yarmouth. It is now situated in an open space, all nearby properties having been demolished.

3. Tradition affirms that the bricked-up portion of the Blackfriars Tower (to be seen on the left of this photograph) conceals the remains of a soldier and his horse.

4. This view of the Blackfriars Tower, taken in the early 1950s, depicts shops and houses which have since been demolished. The tower has now been fully renovated.

5. The custodian of the Caister Roman site, Mr. T. G. Mills, is seen here exhibiting an Anglo-Saxon skull dating from around A.D.600. Experts were amazed at the skull's perfect teeth. On his left is Mr. R. J. Mallett of Runham Vauxhall who discovered a Roman urn in perfect condition, dating from around A.D.300.

6. Dating from 1908, this photograph depicts the old tollhouse dungeons in Middlegate Street. Despite the passage of time they have changed very little.

7.   The famous Kittywitches Row was the narrowest of all Yarmouth's Rows being only 27 in. wide at
the narrowest point. There are several suggestions as to the origin of the Rows. Being built from east
to west, ventilation from the strong sea breezes would help to eliminate disease in the time of the Plague.
The design could also have been part of a defensive measure; in the event of invasion by enemy troops,
one man could have theoretically defended the whole Row. It was demolished by enemy aircraft in 1942.

8. The Fishermen's hospital was erected in 1702 to provide for the needs of 20 'decayed' fishermen. This picture shows the quiet serenity of the cottages in the courtyard. It is interesting to note that Great Yarmouth's only statue stands here.

9. No. 4 South Quay, Great Yarmouth was built in 1596. Tradition states that it was here that the Principals of the Parliamentary army deliberated over plans to execute Charles I in 1648. The famous carved ceiling has been suspended from scores of concealed spring hooks, thereby ensuring that it never collapses.

10. Troll-carts were a unique feature of Yarmouth, designed to negotiate the narrow Rows. The distinguishing feature was the fact that the shafts were attached outside the wheels, facilitating the easy judgement of street widths.

11. Nelson's monument is shown here on Trafalgar Day, during the 1960s, decorated with flags signalling 'Today every man shall do his duty'. Great Yarmouth has the distinction of being the first town to erect a column in honour of Nelson. The foundation stone was laid on 15 August 1817; the plinth faces commemorate four of the ships which participated in the campaign. They are the *Vanguard, Captain, Elephant* and *Victory.*

12. St Nicholas' church, Yarmouth, was built in 1101 by Herbert de Losinga. This photograph shows the church complete with steeple which was used as a landmark for ships passing in the Roads. The church was bombed on 25 June 1942 but has now been restored without the steeple.

13. A special service was held, on the 14th anniversary of the bombing, inside the shell of the church just before rebuilding began. On this occasion the service was attended by the Bishop of Norwich, Dr. P. M. Herbert and the Yarmouth vicar, the Rev. A. G. G. Thurlow.

14. These stones are remnants of masonry left over from the middle ages when the Black Death interrupted the building of the extension to St Nicholas' church. Sailors on leave from their wooden ships anchored in the Roads picked up fragments of this rock which they then used to scour the decks after battle. Hence the saying, to 'holy stone' the ship.

15. St Peter's church was consecrated in August 1833. It temporarily became a 'mother' church following the bombing of St Nicholas' during the Second World War. Ironically, St Peter's claim to fame was being the first church in England to suffer bomb damage during the First World War. The building is now used by the Greek Orthodox Church.

16. The Methodist Temple on Priory Plain is derived from a design, based on a truss (construction of timbers framed together to bridge a space or form a bracket) first used by the Greeks in their temples. Unfortunately this building has been demolished.

17. This unique photograph shows Park Baptist church and Men's Room in 1908. The Men's Room ran a bible class for men of all ages on Sunday afternoons, whilst in the evenings, members could enjoy recreations such as billiards, draughts and dominoes. Note the kiddies' dresses and go-carts.

18. These three cottages in Row 8 became the Methodist chapel where John Wesley preached to 500 people in 1783. Following enemy bombing the entire area was demolished and a new quay constructed.

19. St Andrew's church was once known as the 'Wherryman's church' because it was popular with many seafarers at the end of the 1800s. It has since been demolished.

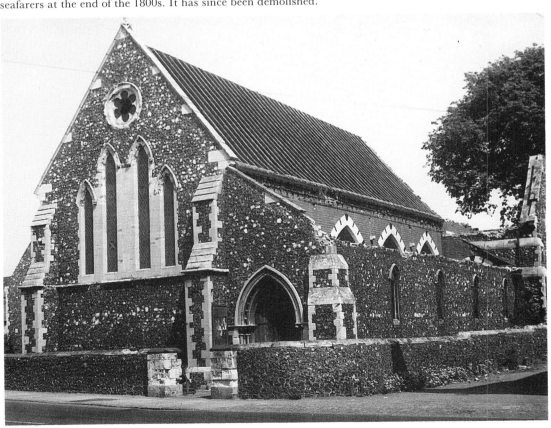

20. This is the last drainage mill to be used in Yarmouth. Based at Ashtree Farm, Great Yarmouth, it continued working until its sails blew off in the storms of 1953.

21. In the foreground of this 1908 picture is the famous Green Cap mill after the disastrous fire. Press's well-known High Mill can be seen in the background.

22. In June 1928, fire destroyed Clark's flour mill and Jewson's wood mill. The fire was spotted on Saturday evening by the town clerk, Mr. M. B. Bowles, who raised the alarm. Fire tenders linked up with water tanks on Southtown Road and the commissioner's tug fought the blaze from the river. It was well into Sunday before the last flames were extinguished; one of the most modern and profitable flour mills in the area had been razed to the ground. Eighteen months later a brand new four-storey mill was opened on the same site.

23. This picture shows the *Albion*, one of the last Norfolk wherries, on Breydon Water.

24.   A peaceful view of Ormesby Broad taken in 1909.

25.   Yachting on Filby Broads.

26. Reminiscent of showboats on American rivers, this scene shows Yarmouth's *Queen of the Broads* steaming upriver at Wroxham, with a full complement of passengers. This was one of the last old steam-driven river boats and has since been broken up for scrap.

27. This picture of 1926 was taken at Caister on Sea. Once an idyllic rural scene, it has now been replaced by a dual carriageway.

28. Harrowing on a farm at Caister adjacent to Caister Castle.

29.   The author is seen here 'driving' an early tractor in 1953.

30.   Finishing the stack at Ashby, 1950.

31. Shopping in Yarmouth market-place in 1909. There are no motor vehicles; only landaus, horse-drawn delivery carts and handbarrows fill the street.

32.   Yarmouth's main street in the summer of 1907. An electric tram can be seen in the centre, whilst to the right a policeman is on point duty; note the white helmet.

33.   These oxen were used as part of an advertising gimmick for Atora beef suet in the 1920s. This photograph was taken in Nelson Road North, almost opposite the old M.G.N. railway exit.

34. Here is a nostalgic picture taken in 1910 showing the second bridge which replaced the famous 'clown' bridge. The old bridge collapsed when a clown from the circus sailed down the river towed by geese. Spectators on the bridge rushed to the other side to obtain a closer view. The bridge collapsed with appalling loss of life.

35. On 25 April 1916, a number of Yarmouth inhabitants gathered at the old Tollhouse on the Suspension Bridge leading to the Acle New Road. They were seeking refuge from bombardment by German warships, and trekked to Norwich for safety. This hexagonal-shaped building, one of two situated at either end of the bridge, measured only three yards across, and was used for 70 years as a boot repair shop.

36.   Taken in the 1920s, this picture shows the old Haven Bridge before it was demolished.

37.   Demolition of Haven Bridge is in progress in this picture of the late 1920s which also shows the temporary bridge in the background. A new bridge was opened by the Prince of Wales (later King Edward VIII) on 21 October 1930. The Southtown or Haven Bridge, as it was called, cost £200,000 to build.

38.   Breydon Bridge was called the 'gateway to the Broads'. It is now demolished and replaced by a modern design.

39.   Hundreds of holiday-makers arriving from the Midlands once thronged this station which was, like many others, closed down and had rails removed through the Beeching cuts. The old M.G.N. railway coalyard was taken over as a bus terminus.

40. Bought for just over a thousand pounds from Torquay, the Winter Gardens were a real bargain. They were later converted into a skating rink and subsequently became an Alpine Biergarten.

41. This group photograph of baby-sitters, wearing 'maxi' dresses, is taken outside the old lamp house at the end of the old Dutch Pier, Gorleston in 1900.

42. Workers at Pretty's corset firm celebrate the coronation of Edward VII, August 1902. On the left is Mr. Daynes the foreman, and on the right is Mrs. Daynes who was the forewoman. The latter used to live in Mill Road, District Cobholm. Whalebone was used to form the supports of the corsets produced at this time.

43. The Royal Naval hospital at Yarmouth in 1958. This fine Georgian building was used as a Naval mental hospital, hence the nautical term, 'Send him to Yarmouth' signifying that the gentleman was in need of 'mental attention'. Nelson is known to have visited wounded from the Battles of the Nile and Copenhagen here. Recent discussions have brought into question the future of the building – will it be pulled down to make way for a car-park or will it be made into a museum?

44. At first glance, this photograph taken on August Bank Holiday in 1894, appears little different from a picture of the same scene today. However, close inspection reveals the absence of gardens on the marine parade, the Empire picture house and amusement arcades. Most noticeable is the total lack of motor vehicles on the Drive.

45. The Promenade, pier and *Cliff Hotel* at Gorleston in 1900. A swimming pool is now situated on the site of the bandstand.

46. Children on the beach near Britannia Pier in 1908.

47. Goat-pulled carts were used as a novelty form of transport for children in 1908. The goats were later replaced by ponies.

48. *(above)* A crowded beach at Yarmouth in 1909. Note the bathing machines near the water's edge.

49. *(above right)* A photograph of Yarmouth beach taken from the jetty, 1909. Note the presence of large numbers of rowing and beach boats, and also the signal station mast on the left. The Aquarium may be seen in the distance.

50. *(right)* These 'modesty' bathing machines are seen here on Yarmouth Sands in 1909. Women normally held on to a long rope attached to the machine to prevent them being swept away by the current. Victorian bathers were clothed in long 'reach-me-downs', extending from the ankle to the throat. The larger machines were used for 'mixed' or family bathing, but they were fully partitioned inside.

51. Since early Edwardian days, summer holiday-makers have always enjoyed a boat trip. Here is a typical scene taken at Great Yarmouth in 1909 showing the *Skylark*.

52. Yarmouth Sands in 1909 with the Britannia Pier in the foreground.

53. This nostalgic picture of Yarmouth, taken in 1910, shows the Revolving Tower, stalls on the beach and numerous rowing boats. The 100-ft. tower had a cage which held passengers and revolved while ascending the tower. It was demolished for scrap during the Second World War.

54. A Punch and Judy show on the Hippodrome forecourt in 1909.

55. Taken in 1910, this picture of Chappell's famous Promenade Concert Party recalls the atmosphere of Edwardian entertainment. The Singer's Ring, the Pierrots and the Promenade concerts took place near the site of today's Marina.

56. Summer visitors crowding Chappell's Promenade Concert on Yarmouth beach in 1910.

57. The bandstand, in the Wellington Pier Gardens, was a rendezvous for visitors and locals alike. The top of the bandstand was embellished with muses each with a different musical instrument. It has now been replaced by a model village and an outdoor skating rink.

58. This 1896 view shows the entrance to the old Britannia Pier.

59. The ornate pavilion of the Britannia Pier was built by Boulton & Paul of Norwich for a total cost of £16,000. Opened in 1902, it burnt down only seven years later. The 'dome' and four minarets stand out in this photograph of 1908.

60.   On 22 December 1909 the Britannia Pier Pavilion caught fire and was destroyed.

61.   Tragedy swept the pier for a second time on 20 April 1954. All that was saved from the flames was this miniature train.

62. This 1920s photograph shows an old solid-tyred charabanc on Theatre Plain, Great Yarmouth. A canvas hood would be rolled over the passengers when it rained.

63. The Venetian Waterways at Great Yarmouth were built in the 1920s to relieve unemployment at the time.

64. One of the famous Belle boats passing Jewson's timber yard in the 1920s.

65. Children's rides in Wellington Pier Gardens in the 1940s.

66. Swing-boats at the annual Spring Fair at Great Yarmouth. Showmen gathered together here before separating to give shows to other small towns and villages. The steeple of St Nicholas' church can be seen in the background.

67. The last of the pleasure sailing boats, the *Cambria 5*, is seen here near the Britannia Pier in 1930. She was one of a number of former beach yawls which were refitted with cutter rig sails for easier handling. On one occasion the *Cambria* stuck fast on Scroby Sandbank whilst loaded with passengers, and had to be pulled free by over a dozen motor boats.

68. Many visitors marvelled at the creations made by the sand artist, Frederick Bultitude, on Great Yarmouth beach. From the 1930s onwards he modelled many scenes using just sand and water, including sagas of 'the covered waggon', the soldier and his wounded horse, and Christie the murderer.

69. A happy family scene on Gorleston beach in the 1930s.

70. Much publicity has surrounded Gorleston's 'lost beach'. This picture of the mid-1950s shows a fairly large expanse of sand and the sea in the distance.

71. By contrast this picture, dating from the mid-1960s, shows a well-populated and much smaller beach.

72.   This picture taken at 3 o'clock on August Bank Holiday, 1953, shows the sands near Britannia Pier packed with holiday-makers and day-trippers.

73. People overflowed from the beach to the gardens during the resort's most popular years.

74. The 'Cosies', Gorleston Pier, were popular with both summer visitors and locals who dozed, read, fished and, at night, cuddled! Unfortunately, the pier has been stripped of all character, having been faced with concrete.

75. Mr. R. C. Soames, the lighthouse keeper, is shown here at the end of Gorleston Pier in the 1950s. The removal of the third pennant denotes that the water at the bar has dropped a foot. The lighthouse and the signals no longer exist.

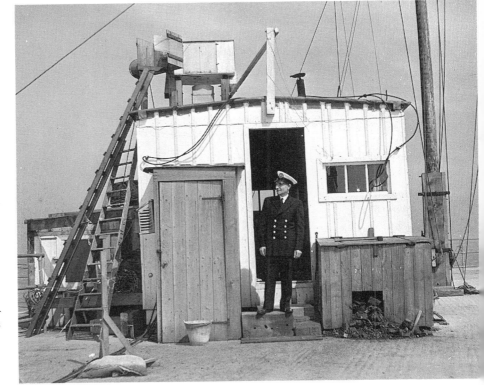

76. After over a century of use the pepperpot lamphouse at the end of Gorleston Pier was replaced in 1963 by this temporary hut. The old lighthouse had witnessed the arrival of over one thousand fishing vessels in Yarmouth, numerous shipwrecks and timber-carrying barquentines from Baltic ports. Mr. Hudson is standing in the doorway.

77. The Gorleston lifeguard, Mr. Tom Collins, is holding a baby seal which had come ashore from Scroby Sandbank. This seal was so young that its umbilical cord was still attached – a rare occurrence.

78. Holiday-makers on the old Dutch Pier, watching the boats come in.

79. Punch and Judy show on the beach in 1953. The third Pavilion Theatre at the end of the pier was burnt down in 1954. The star billing was for the comedian, the late Frankie Howerd.

80. A bird's eye view of Yarmouth front showing its open-air swimming pool, Wellington Pier in the background, and Nelson's jetty in the centre. Two years after this photograph was taken the entire complex was demolished to make way for a new development.

81. Gorleston beach was once renowned for its sands. However, since the erection of the new Gorleston Pier, the sea has encroached, at times reaching the sea wall itself.

82.   Jonah, a rorqual whale measuring some 65 ft. in length and weighing 69 tons, was exhibited at the pleasure beach for two days in the 1940s. Other whales found their way to Yarmouth including one in the early 1900s. It swam upriver and was chased by excited boatmen before it was captured and stuffed by 'John Knowlittle'.

83.   This is the last photograph to be taken of Arthur H. Patterson, a local character known as 'John Knowlittle'. An artist, historian, author, lecturer, naturalist and ornithologist, his local claim to fame was as the taxidermist who stuffed the aforementioned whale.

84.   A talent competition was held on August Bank Holiday 1955 at the Marina. The host, Neville Bishop, is introducing the next act on stage watched by hundreds. The Marina itself was built in 1937 at a cost of £12,000 and was thought to be ideal for band concerts, stage entertainments or even conferences. Having been used for such diverse entertainments as wrestling and Wild West shows, the Marina was considered for redevelopment as a dolphinarium. It has now been demolished and transformed into a multi-million pound leisure complex.

85 & 86.   In 1926 Great Yarmouth was selected as the location for a film entitled *The Rolling Road*, based on a novel by Boyd Cable. The cast and crew stayed at the *Queen's Hotel*, now the *New Beach*, opposite Britannia Pier. Many of the film's sequences were filmed in and around the town and local inhabitants were used as extras. A picturesque sailing barque, the *Shakespeare*, was specially chartered and, renamed the *Gleam*, was used in many of the sequences. When the film was released and shown in local cinemas the audience were amazed to see the golden sands of Yarmouth adorned with tropical palm trees. Amongst the many incidents to be filmed was the rescue of the heroine, Flora le Breton, from the sea by the hero, Carlyle Blackwell. However, the October sea proved too cold for Flora, clad in the first 'bikini' – two pieces of her dress – to be seen in Great Yarmouth. She had to be rescued in real life when she lost consciousness in the freezing water.

87. Miss Yarmouth competition in August 1956. There were 32 entrants in the competition held at the Marina.

88. This picture, taken in 1961, celebrates 200 years of the bathing machine.

89. This unique photograph shows the development of the bathing costume, from the bodice-pantaloon and frilled bonnet (in the centre) to the modern bikini costume.

90. Children playing on Gorleston Sands in 1945.

91. Yarmouth's first cinema, the Gem, was opened by Charles 'Cocky' Cochrane in 1908. It later became the Windmill Theatre and now houses a museum.

92. The Royal Aquarium was used initially, as the name suggests, as an aquarium. It was later converted into a theatre which hosted touring West End operas and musical comedies. It then had the first Cinemascope screen in East Anglia, *The Robe* being one of the top ten box office hits of all time.

93. Mr. Frank Ginnett, the ringmaster, is seen posing outside Yarmouth's permanent circus on its re-opening after the Second World War. The circus was well known for its sunken ring – one of only two in the country.

94. Dancing bears at the circus – such spectacles are now outlawed.

95.   Wellington Pier was opened in 1854 and the Pavilion was added in 1903, taking only two months to build. During the First World War troops used the theatre to put on wonderful performances. This picture was taken in 1952. For the last twenty years or so the theatre has featured a number of famous television celebrities.

96.   The Marina in its heyday in 1953.

97. The scenic railway with its fairy castle was situated on the pleasure beach and was the largest in Europe. It is now a rollercoaster with American-influenced visual effects.

98. Members of Hengler's Circus in 1923 are entertaining holiday-makers in the street, in an effort to raise money for a hospital on Marine Parade.

99. Bobby Roberts, seen here aged six, was the world's youngest clown. He first put on clown's make-up at the age of four when he appeared in his father's circus, Roberts Brothers. This picture was taken on Beaconsfield recreation ground, Yarmouth.

100. The popular pianist Russ Conway is seen here, in 1961, surrounded by autograph-hunting fans at Wellington Pier.

101. The four Gibson sisters appeared at the Royal Aquarium during the summer seasons in the 1960s.

102. This gipsy encampment had just arrived in Yarmouth in August 1949 after a film had been made about them at the Elstree Studios.

103. This gipsy family is camping near the racecourse, August 1949.

104. Pictured here in 1970 is 'Peggotty's hut', erected for a film production of Dickens' *David Copperfield* near Kessingland.

105. The paddle tug *Gleaner* towing six Scottish fishing vessels, *c*.1909.

106. This historic picture of 1909 shows fifies and zulus (types of wooden fishing vessel), which came from Banff and Fraserburgh, Scotland for the autumn fishing season.

107.   This is a 1909 view of a packed fish wharf at Yarmouth, featuring the swills (receptacles for herrings) which were unique to Yarmouth and Lowestoft. The record season for fish landing was in 1913 when 835 million herrings, weighing 157,000 tons, were landed by 1,163 Yarmouth fish wharf vessels. The fish were sold for about one million pounds. At that time one could buy a 'string' of herrings (about twenty) for a 'tanner', 6d. in old money.

108. *(above)* A fleet of old wooden
steam-powered Yarmouth fishing
drifters, none of which now exist.
The steel-hulled *Lydia Eva* is
preserved. This photograph was
taken in the late 1920s.

109. *(above right)* Tugs were used
for towing and salvage and this
busy scene at the harbour bend
shows a number of them pulling
steamships with cargoes of timber.
Fishing luggers, a Thames sailing
barge and steam herring drifters
can also be seen in this turn of the
century photograph.

110. *(right)* Scottish and local
fishing drifters queue alongside
each other at the harbour to enter
the port.

111. Typical Scottish fisherfolk are busy packing barrels with alternate layers of herring and salt for export on the South Denes in 1926. The weekly wage was £2 with a bonus of 2s. 6d. for every barrel filled by a team of three.

112. These Scottish luggers are being towed out of Yarmouth harbour, *c*.1909.

113. The local tug *Richard Lee Barber* is pictured towing the Yarmouth-built London barge *Greenhithe* upriver. Scottish fishing vessels are assembled in the background. Most of the buildings shown were destroyed by enemy action during the Second World War.

114.   This is an imposing 1920s picture of steam fishing drifters which have made the long trip from Peterhead (P.D.), Inverness (I.N.S.), Fraserburgh (F.R.) and Banff (B.F.), and are moored at Yarmouth quayside for the 'Sabbath rest'. They took over from the old brown-sailed luggers and smacks, and were in turn replaced by diesel-powered boats. The *Lydia Eva* is the only steam fishing drifter left in existence.

115.   When Yarmouth's fishing industry was at its peak there were nearly 2,000 fishing vessels using the port. The river would be so packed with boats that one could cross from bank to bank by clambering from deck to deck. The town hall may be seen in the background of this view of the river.

116. This photograph taken in 1949 shows Nelson's column standing sentinel over a huge stack of barrels which, when packed, were exported to the Low Countries.

117. Ken Goddard of the Pathé News is filming the fishing fleet at Yarmouth on Trafalgar Day 1957. English and Scottish fishing craft stretched in a line for seven and a half miles passed a saluting base opposite Britannia Pier. The film was shown at local cinemas on the Pathé News (a popular cinema information service, with its 'crowing cock' emblem, which started in 1908).

118. The old fish wharf at Yarmouth is shown in this view of 1945. All the sheds and buildings on the right have now been demolished leaving an open area.

119. This cage-like structure, aboard a ship moored at South Quay, was erected to prevent thousands of empty barrels falling overboard.

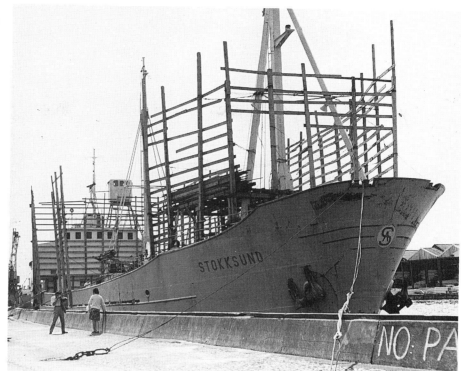

120. Visitors to Yarmouth in the 1950s are watching the Scottish gutting-girls at work during the autumn fishing period.

121. In 1950 South Denes was open land where under the terms of a royal charter fishermen dried their nets, and people indulged in recreational activities such as football, kite-flying and picnicking. Today this area is totally covered with factories and offices belonging to the sea gas and oil companies.

122. After the fish merchants had stopped buying for the day, surplus herring – tons of it on this day in 1954 – was sent to the herring reduction factory for conversion into meal and oil. The factory, seen here on the far right, was eventually demolished and a B.P. oil company building was erected in its place.

123.   Exporting cattle to the continent from Gorleston quayside in April 1965. An electric goad was used to persuade the frightened animals to go on board.

124.   This is the old
shipyard of Hewitts,
Gorleston. In the late
19th century, when this
photograph was taken, the
only machinery was a crude
lathe and all the work was
done manually. A capstan
worked by a horse would
provide the hauling
mechanism, and a block and
tackle fixed to a spar would
swing the largest piece of
timber into position. The
sawyers in the saw pit in the
foreground are cutting out
the strakes from huge logs
brought to the yard by horse-
drawn 'drugs'.

125.   A nostalgic picture of Yarmouth quayside, 1896. In the background, to the left, one can see Press's High Mill. The Belle paddle steamer, on the extreme right, disgorged London trippers whilst the Bessey and Palmer collier brigs brought coal to the port. The crowd is drawn by the famous Barnum and Bailey's circus parade.

126. The *Success* came from Botany Bay and was fitted up as a convict ship museum. She was on show at Yarmouth in 1903.

127.   A Bessey and Palmer collier being towed up the Yarmouth River by the screw tug *Fastnet* in 1910. The old racecourse on the South Denes can be seen in the background, where factories, a power station and oil containers now stand.

128. This crew was photographed at the beginning of the century. Note the unseamanlike 'bowler' hat. On the right is the man-operated pump used for discharging bilge water.

129. This picture shows a wide variety of shipping in Yarmouth harbour. On the left is the coaster *Ipswich Trader*. The three-masted sailing ship in the centre is the *Linguard* which was used as a store by the Germans in the Second World War. Parts of her are still preserved in Norway. On the right is the paddle steamer *United Service* which had a number of uses including being used as a pleasure vessel for holiday-makers. During the Second World War she was sunk in the harbour by a warship, was subsequently raised and sent to a breaker's yard.

130. One of Yarmouth's lightships. Such vessels were used to control and guide the flow of shipping; they have since become obsolete with automatic buoys used in their place.

131. Mr. W. Gowing is overhauling one of the numerous buoys brought in by the Trinity vessel *Warden*. Such work took place on Trinity House Quay in Great Yarmouth.

132.   This picture of 1909 captures several different types of vessel moored at the harbour, including a turret ship, sailing barge, paddle tug, sailing wherry and windjammer.

133.   A London barge at the quayside, 1926.

134.   An animated river scene at Yarmouth, showing a lighter being loaded on the starboard side of the steamer. Others are unloading on the port side, traversing long, narrow gangway planks while having long lengths of wood on their shoulders. These would then be stacked in orderly piles at Jewson's Timber Yard. Note the 'platform' on the left – part of a scheme to restore the quayside with new piles.

135.   A holiday pleasure craft taking visitors on a sea trip in the 1950s.

136. Yarmouth town hall presides over this riverside vista. This picture is unique in that it depicts six vessels all of which have now disappeared from the scene. The lifeboat making its way upriver is carrying a B.B.C. television crew.

137. A scene at North Quay showing the humble 'wolder' or shrimp boat alongside the more modern motor cruisers and yachts, c.1950. The suspension bridge in the background replaced that which had collapsed on 2 May 1845.

138. The coaster *Severity* is shown here in the stocks at Fellow's shipyard in March 1954. She was launched only two months later. The yard has since been roofed and wholly enclosed. Shipbuilding was once a thriving industry in Yarmouth; shipyards were situated all along the quayside and their sailing barques, brigs and lifeboats were exported throughout the world.

139. These four river steamers made regular trips from South Quay to Gorleston and back: the *Yarmouth*, *Resolute*, *South Town* and *Cobholm* were commonly called the 'backwards and forwards' steamers, because they never turned round as ordinary ships do. The *Yarmouth* is now preserved with other unique craft in St Katharine's Dock, London, but all four are sadly missed by those locals and summer visitors who remember them from their childhood days.

140.   This 1950s view along Yarmouth quayside shows railway trucks laden with coal for the steam drifters. Gone are the famous 'Defoe trees', the coal trucks and lines, and the Trinity house tender *Warden* from which this photo was taken.

141. The *Beauchamp* capsized on 13 November 1901 with the loss of nine lives. Many willing helpers are shown hauling in the stricken lifeboat.

142. On 4 November 1902 the schooner *Maggie Williams* was wrecked on the breakwater at Gorleston. The top of one of her masts can still be seen at low tide today.

143. This 1903 photograph shows the old Yarmouth lifeboats *John Burch* and *Duff* in the shed (now a grotto). In 1919 the station was closed and Gorleston assumed all responsibility for this part of the coast. Note the tall observation tower on the right where a lookout watched for ships in trouble.

144. The crew of the *John Burch* are posing with their lifeboat in 1908. So numerous were the crew that there seemed to be little room for the rescued.

145. Until 1914 horses were used for transporting and launching the lifeboats at Yarmouth. Six horses are shown here pulling the Gorleston lifeboat *Leicester* on the South Denes. In all there were three lifeboats bearing the name of 'Leicester'; between the three of them they saved a total of 203 lives.

146. In 1909 Lifeboat Day was held during Regatta Week (end of August and the beginning of September). This picture shows the *Worchester Cadet* on its iron-wheeled carriage.

147.   On 10 December 1927 the *Sussex Belle* was anchored in Yarmouth Roads to ride out the gale. Her anchors dragged, however, and she was driven aground near the harbour entrance. Waves broke over the vessel and flooded both cabin and forecastle, thus preventing crew from sending out distress signals. Their cries for help remained unheard until a lull in the storm when the rocket brigade arrived and a successful rescue was effected.

148.   Laden with timber, the steamship *Oscar* burst into flames off Yarmouth on 19 December 1927. It burnt for five days and nights until it was sunk by a controlled explosion carried out by Trinity House. The crew had been rescued by the Gorleston lifeboat under cox William Fleming.

149. Stacks of timber from the burnt-out *Oscar* were washed ashore in great heaps.

150. This 1926 view shows the old lifeboatmen's lookout at Caister. The 'Gap' and longshore boats can be seen in the foreground, with *Seek and Find* on the right, from which seven fishermen were rescued by Skipper Woodhouse. Today, this scene is completely changed.

151. The *Elizabeth Simpson* began life in 1888 as a lifeboat, serving in this capacity until 1939, having cost £300 to build and equip. In 1926, she was converted to motor power by Newman of Gorleston. After 51 years of service she became a pleasure cruiser on the Norfolk Broads.

152. Mr. William Fleming, a former lifeboat coxswain and Gorleston personality, is photographed on his 84th birthday. He was cabin boy in a fishing boat at the age of 12 and a lifeboatman at 19 years of age. When Mr. Fleming retired in 1934, he had 48 years of service with the R.N.L.I., and had helped to save 1,188 lives. He was awarded the Institution's gold medal in 1922, bronze medal in 1925 and silver medal in 1927. He received a silver watch from the Queen of Holland for his fearless seamanship in going to the rescue of the Dutch steamer *Georgia* and was also awarded the O.B.E. and the George Cross. He died aged 89 in September 1954.

153. This dramatic photograph taken in September 1933 shows the burnt-out hull of the steamer *Porthcawl*. She drifted ashore having burned at sea for four days and nights.

154. The 18 November 1936 was a disastrous day for shipping in the Yarmouth region. Fearsome storms battered the coast. The Scottish drifter *Pitgavenny* ran ashore at Gorleston, whilst the drifter *Olive Branch* capsized with the loss of all hands. Later the wreck was washed up on Kessingland beach. The Glasgow steamship *Yewbank* was driven ashore at Horsey, and the *Sapphire* had to be towed to Lowestoft. Two members of a lifeboat crew were swept overboard but were saved, and a barge the *Lady Gwynfred* was driven ashore at Runton.

155. A naval fleet visited Yarmouth in 1903 comprising the *Majestic, Mars, Jupiter, Prince George, Hannibal, Suties, Doris, Prometheus* and *Magnificent*. One of these warships can be seen in the background.

156.   The frigate H.M.S. *Yarmouth*, shown here, is the sixth vessel to be named after the town. She is 370 ft. long, with a 41 ft. beam, 13 ft. draught and a displacement of 2,162 tons.

157.   The big guns and turrets of the old three-funnelled H.M.S. *Norfolk*, photographed off the coast of Yarmouth.

158.   Yarmouth was one of the first towns in Britain to suffer air-raid damage. On 19 January 1915, a Zeppelin raid on Yarmouth caused the death of Sam Smith, aged 50, and Miss Martha Taylor, aged 72. This picture shows some of the damage caused to St Peters Plain.

159. Further damage caused
by the Zeppelin raid,
January 1915.

160. Shown here is one of
the Zeppelins which flew
over Yarmouth on that
fateful day. Each was nearly
600 ft. long and 40 ft. in
diameter and carried a crew
of forty.

161. This tank was used as a war memorial after the First World War and was situated on the Hall Quay, Great Yarmouth. Thousands of schoolchildren thronged the streets to watch this awkward vehicle destroying the road surface with its caterpillar tracks as it was finally manoeuvred into position on a wedge-shaped concrete base.

162. The destruction caused by Second World War air-raids is evident in this view of the Middlegate Street area.

163. In 1940, in order to prevent enemy troops landing, the centre portion of Britannia Pier was blown up, whilst the rest of the beach was mined and strewn with rolls of barbed wire. This picture shows the narrow gangway between the two sections to facilitate the use of the pier end as a look-out point.

164. This picture, taken at the Beaconsfield recreation ground, shows the first balloon ascent in the area.

165. Air sheds on the South Denes were formally the centre for the Royal Naval Air Service. It is said that pilots took off from here and brought down a German Zeppelin during the First World War. This picture dates from 1930.

166. Mr. A. W. Fairlie making the first parachute descent in the area, 12 September 1929.

167. Seen here after his successful parachute descent is Mr. A. W. Fairlie.

168. In 1929, Sir Alan Cobham brought his flying circus to Gorleston and Yarmouth. He flew his special plane *Youth of Britain* in an attempt to make the younger generation 'air conscious'.

169. Sir Alan Cobham's aeroplane *Youth of Britain* on South Denes, 1929. Flights were given to lucky schoolchildren.

170.   In 1932 the Yarmouth Mayor, Mr. E. Middleton, and the Deputy Town Clerk, Mr. A. J. Reeves, gave a civic
welcome to the officers and crew of four flying boats which had landed half a mile from shore at Yarmouth.

171.   Rowing and motor boats did a roaring trade taking sightseers to view the flying boats, 1932.

172.   In the 1960s, huge barge platforms arrived at Yarmouth for the oil rig companies.

173. *Mr. Louie* was one of the many rigs used to drill for natural gas and oil. To the right of the rig may be seen a departing supply ship.

174. In 1966 pipes for the new North Sea gas industry were prepared and reinforced at Gorleston.

175. A German supply ship, the *Fangturm*, named after one of the towers at Bremen, is seen here entering Yarmouth harbour.

176. Looking like a monster from another world, this huge suction pipe is being repaired at Gas House Quay, Great Yarmouth. With a combination of water and compressed air, it was used to make a 'bed' 10 ft. deep, on which to lay the treated pipes from the oil rig to Bacton, Norfolk.

177. A number of Americans worked in association with the rigs, and Yarmouth's natives were not at all surprised to see a large banner fronting Southtown railway station, with the words 'Santa Fe Oilfield Trading Company Ltd.'. The station has now been demolished.

178. The huge floods of January 1953 wrought tremendous damage upon Yarmouth jetty. This is all that remained of the jetty.

179. To minimise damage from the 1953 floods, sandbags were filled to breach the gaps in the broken walls of the river at Breydon. The Marina in the background is now demolished.

180. This was all that remained of the swimming pool on the seafront following the floods.